KINDERGARTEN
LEARNING MATHEMATICS FROM PICTURES TO WORDS

AUTHORS
DR. EDWARD C. HAYNIE
LAMAR HART

Table of Contents

Acknowledgements

This booklet is dedicated to Dr. Joyce Taylor Haynie for her interest, support, and belief in STEM (Science, Technology, Engineering, and Mathematics) and to Ethan Haynie who strongly encouraged the writing of this booklet. He believed that having strong skills in mathematics helped propel his career success in the field of Architecture.

Great appreciation is extended to Edward C. Haynie, Jr. for his marketing skills and to Jibri Robinson in recognition of his artistic skills in preparation of this booklet. Captain Patrick R. Haynie has been an inspiration while serving as an officer in the U.S. Marines.

Overview

This booklet presents a way for scholars to learn mathematical words from pictures. Word development is fundamentally used to improve reading, writing, mathematics, and science skills. We encourage all parents and teachers to emphasize learning in these areas for their young scholars. The pictures represent mathematical words that students need to know and understand to prepare for reading and completing word problems.

Goals for Mathematics in Kindergarten

- Enhance students' knowledge, understanding and skills related to mathematics sight words.
- Help children to develop mathematic reasoning, skills, and enhance their ability to solve practical problems.
- Contribute to children's conceptual understanding of the world around them.
- Foster the development of positive attitudes in studying mathematics.

Kindergarten: How Children Learn Mathematics From Pictures to Words

Children learn mathematics concepts from both the informal, unstructured experiments in their environment and the more formal, structured educational setting known as school.

The objectives of this booklet are to assist teachers to understand how children learn basic mathematics skills and solve problems.

Learning Theories Applied to Mathematics for Kindergarten:

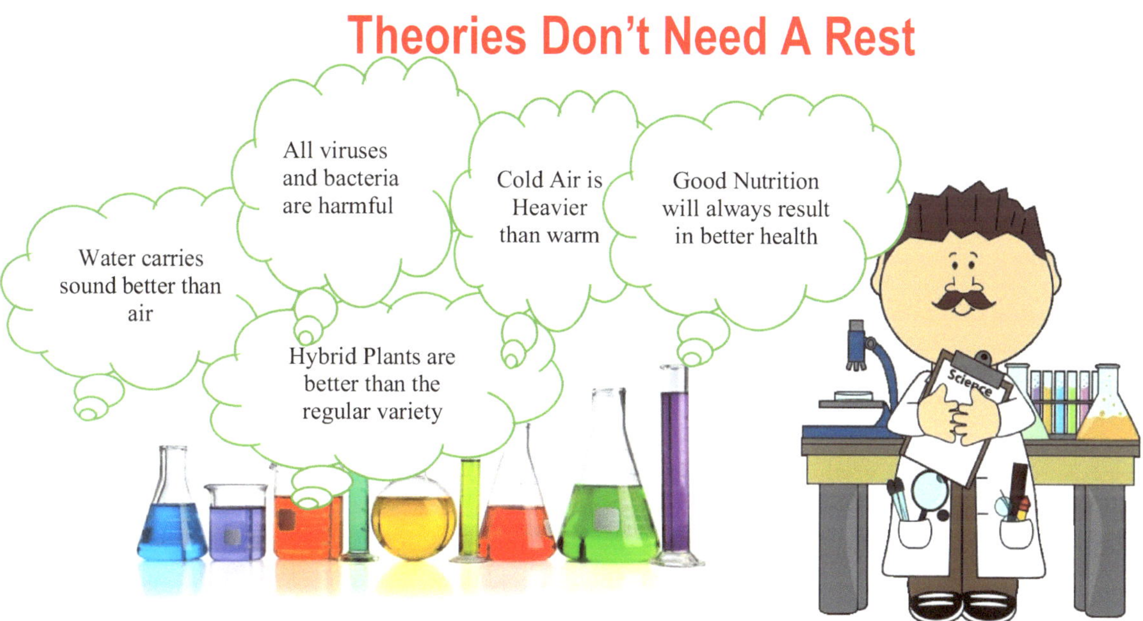

The Constructivists/Cognitive (Learning in action)
- Constructivists believe that children must be allowed to experiment physically with the things around them if they are to learn. They believe active learning builds mental structures.
- Jean Piaget:
  - Theory is age and stage related, which means that students go through definite developmental stages in their lives. Each stage must be completed before a person can attain the next stage.
  - Preoperational stage (2 years old – 6 years old) Acting on Reality
    - Children know that objects exist outside of themselves, recognize that objects have properties, and will use words to tell you so.

Kindergarten

The aim in Learning Mathematics From Pictures to Words is to build mathematics skills for Kindergarten scholars.
- Connecting pictures with words to familiar objects
- Placing pictures with words together
- Recognizing familiar pictures to words

Kindergarten Common Core Standards

The Kindergarten common core standards provide students with a firm foundation while learning whole numbers, addition, and subtraction. As scholars progress, these standards prepare them for enhanced for learning and application of more demanding mathematics concepts and procedures.

Research supports the recommendation that efforts to enhance knowledge and skills in mathematics for Kindergarten should focus on the number core; learning how numbers correspond to quantities, and learning how to put numbers together and to take them apart (the beginning of addition and subtraction). These are complicated ideas that take time to learn. Research also suggests that without these critical building blocks in place, mathematics performance will suffer in later grades.

COUNTING AND CARDINALITY
- KNOW NUMBER NAMES AND THE COUNT SEQUENCE.
- COUNT TO TELL THE NUMBER OF OBJECTS.
- COMPARE NUMBERS.

OPERATIONS AND ALGEBRAIC THINKING
- UNDERSTAND ADDITION AS PUTTING TOGETHER AND ADDING TO,
- AND UNDERSTAND SUBTRACTION AS TAKING APART AND TAKING FROM.

NUMBER AND OPERATIONS IN BASE TEN
- WORK WITH NUMBERS 11-19 TO GAIN FOUNDATIONS FOR PLACE VALUE. MEASUREMENT AND DATA
- DESCRIBE AND COMPARE MEASURABLE ATTRIBUTES.
- CLASSIFY OBJECTS AND COUNT THE NUMBER OF OBJECTS IN EACH CATEGORY

GEOMETRY
- IDENTIFY AND DESCRIBE SHAPES.
- ANALYZE, COMPARE, CREATE, AND COMPOSE SHAPES.

MATHEMATICAL PRACTICES
- MAKE SENSE OF PROBLEMS AND PERSEVERE IN SOLVING THEM.
- REASON ABSTRACTLY AND QUANTITATIVELY.
- CONSTRUCT VIABLE ARGUMENTS AND CRITIQUE THE REASONING OF OTHERS.
- MODEL WITH MATHEMATICS.
- USE APPROPRIATE TOOLS STRATEGICALLY.
- ATTEND TO PRECISION.
- LOOK FOR AND MAKE USE OF STRUCTURE.
- LOOK FOR AND EXPRESS REGULARITY IN REPEATED REASONING

Words to Know

1. One fewer
2. One more
3. Two fewer
4. Two more
5. About the same
6. Above (over)
7. Add
8. Addition sentence
9. As long as (same length as)
10. As many as
11. As short as
12. As tall as
13. Balance
14. Behind
15. Below (under)
16. Circle
17. Cone
18. Corner
19. Count
20. Count by 10's
21. Count by 2's
22. Cube
23. Cylinder
24. Difference
25. Different
26. Does not belong
27. Edge
28. Empty
29. Equal sign
30. Fewer
31. Flat surface
32. Full
33. Graph
34. Greater
35. Growing pattern
36. Heavier (weighs more) than
37. Hexagon
38. Holds less hold more
39. Hundred chart
40. In front of
41. Inside
42. Join
43. Least
44. Left
45. Less than
46. Lighter (weighs less) than
47. Longer than
48. Longest
49. Minus sign
50. More than
51. Most
52. Number line
53. Number story
54. Numbers
55. On (on top of)
56. Order
57. Outside
58. Over
59. Part
60. Picture graph
61. Plus sign
62. Real graph
63. Rectangle
64. Right
65. Roll
66. Same
67. Same number as
68. Same shape
69. Same size
70. Shorter than
71. Shortest
72. Side
73. Sort
74. Sphere
75. Square
76. Subtract (take away)
77. Subtraction sentence
78. Sum
79. Taller than
80. Tallest
81. Triangle
82. Under
83. Whole

Kindergarten Topics

The following is a list of essential topics based on curriculum standards that students in Kindergarten should know and understand.

- ONE TO FIVE
- COMPARING AND ORDERING 0 TO 5
- SIX TO TEN
- COMPARING AND ORDERING NUMBERS 0 TO 10
- NUMBERS TO 20
- NUMBERS TO 100
- UNDERSTANDING ADDITION
- UNDERSTANDING SUBTRACTION
- MORE ADDITION AND SUBTRACTION
- COMPOSING NUMBERS 11 TO 19
- DECOMPOSING NUMBERS 11 TO 19
- MEASUREMENT
- SORTING, CLASSIFYING, COUNTING, AND CATEGORIZING DATA
- IDENTIFYING AND DESCRIBING SHAPES
- POSITION AND LOCATION OF SHAPES
- ANALYZING, COMPARING, AND COMPOSING SHAPES

Learning Mathematics from Pictures to Words

1. 1 FEWER 	6. ABOVE (OVER) 
2. 1 MORE 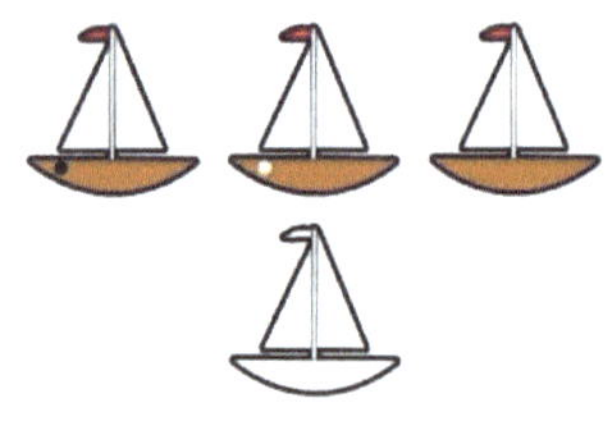	7. ADD 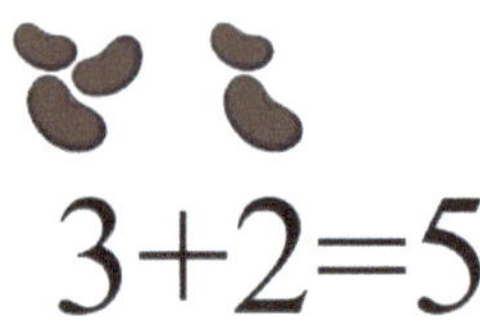 $$3+2=5$$
3. 2 FEWER 	8. ADDITION SENTENCE $$9+2=11$$
4. 2 MORE 	9. AS LONG AS (SAME LENGTH AS) 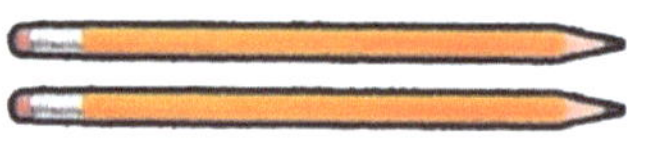
5. ABOUT THE SAME 	10. AS MANY AS 

11. AS SHORT AS	16. CIRCLE
12. AS TALL AS	17. CONE
13. BALANCE	18. CORNER
14. BEHIND	19. COUNT
15. BELOW	20. COUNT BY 10'S

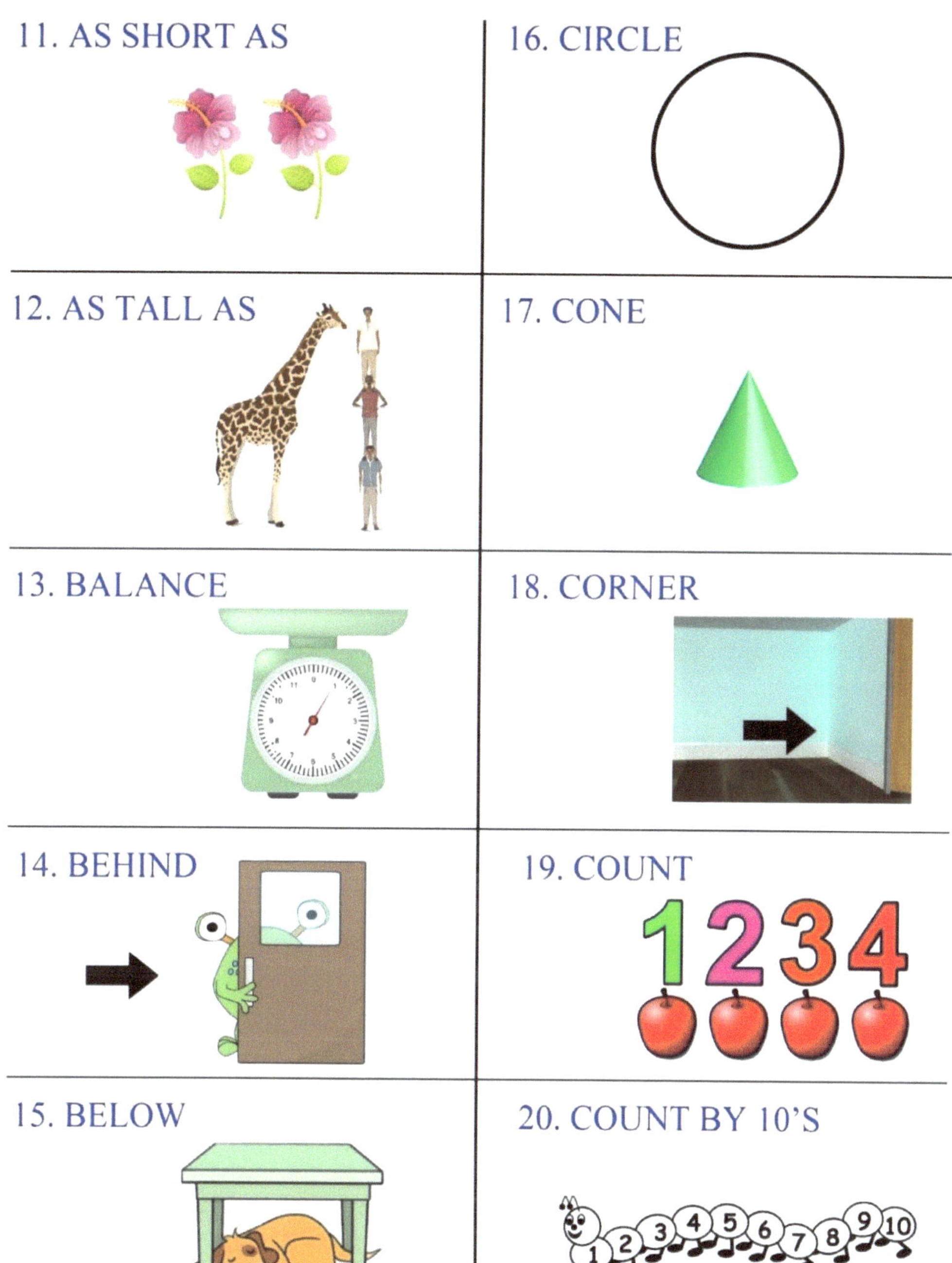

21. COUNT BY 2S	26. DOES NOT BELONG
6 8 10 12 14 16	
22. CUBE	27. EDGE
23. CYLINDER	28. EMPTY
24. DIFFERENCE	29. EQUAL SIGN
25. DIFFERENT	30. FEWER

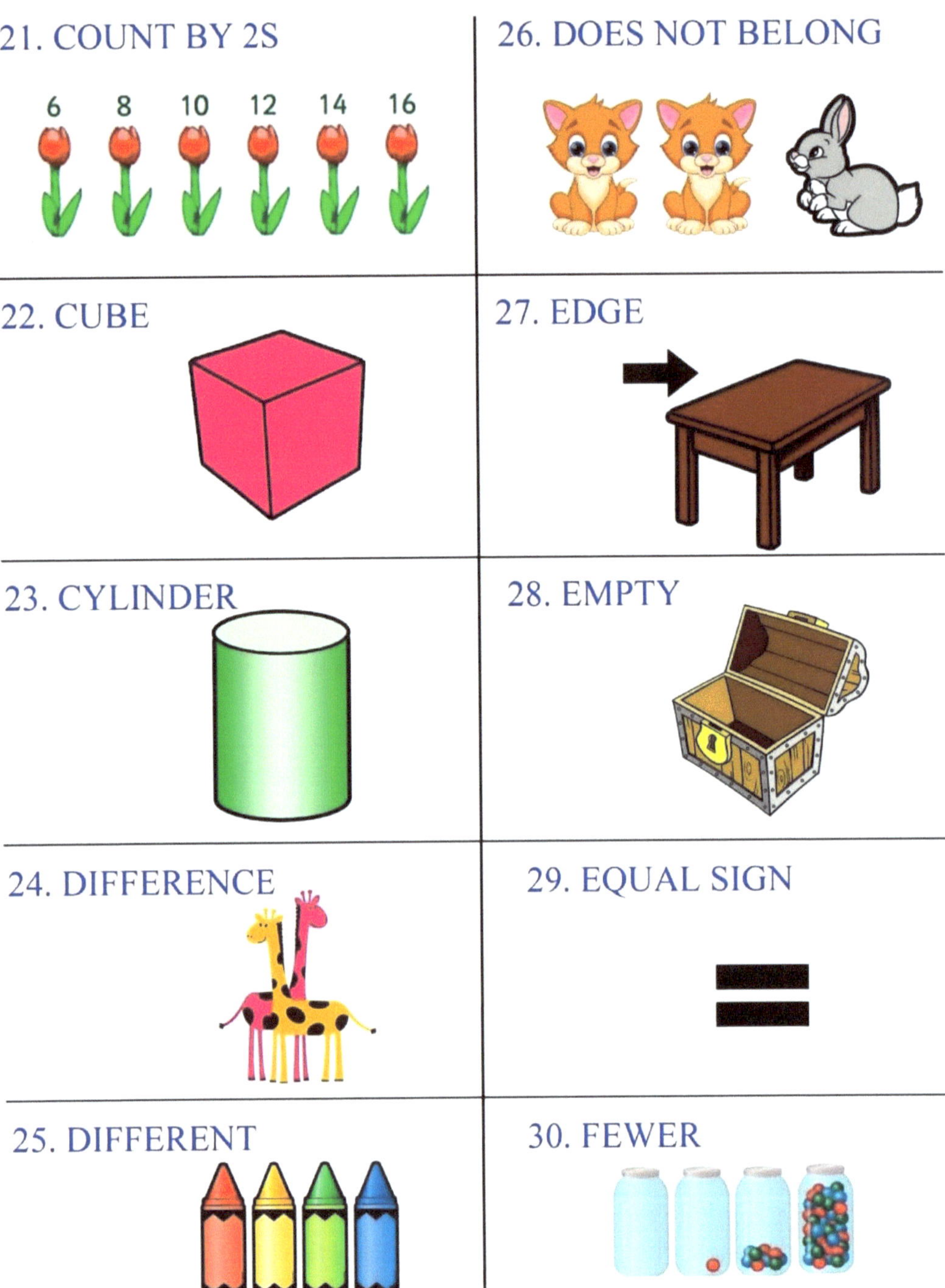

32. FULL

37. HEXAGON

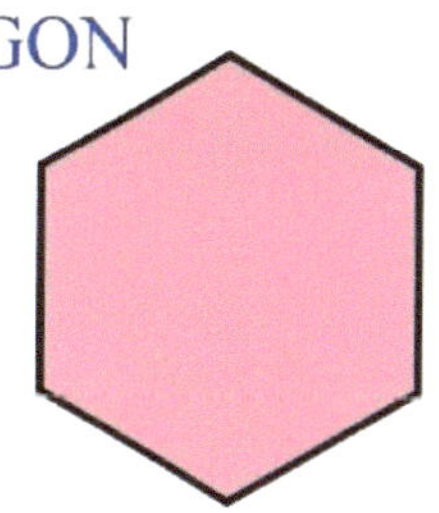

33. GRAPH

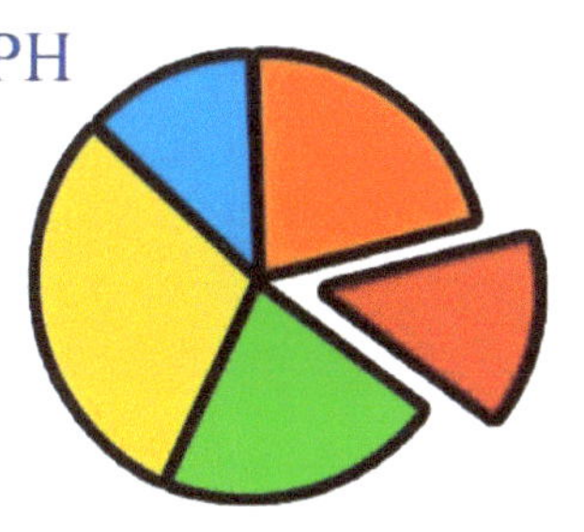

38. HOLDS MORE

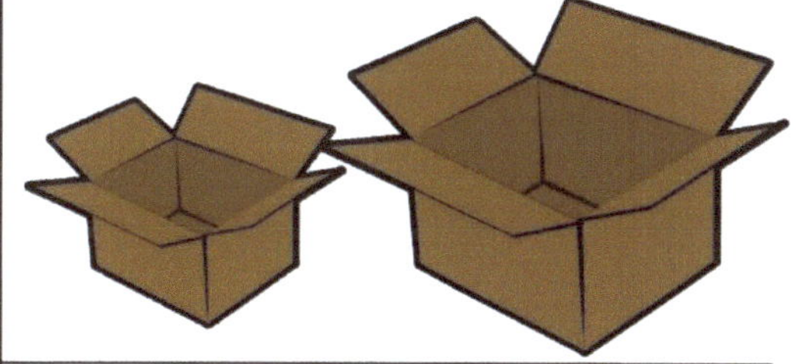

34. GREATER

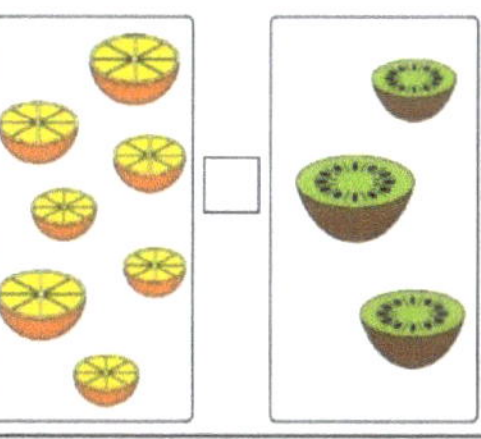

39. HUNDRED CHART

1	2	3	4	5	6	7	8	9	10
11	12	13	14	15	16	17	18	19	20
21	22	23	24	25	26	27	28	29	30
31	32	33	34	35	36	37	38	39	40
41	42	43	44	45	46	47	48	49	50
51	52	53	54	55	56	57	58	59	60
61	62	63	64	65	66	67	68	69	70
71	72	73	74	75	76	77	78	79	80
81	82	83	84	85	86	87	88	89	90
91	92	93	94	95	96	97	98	99	100

35. GROWING PATTERN

40. IN FRONT OF

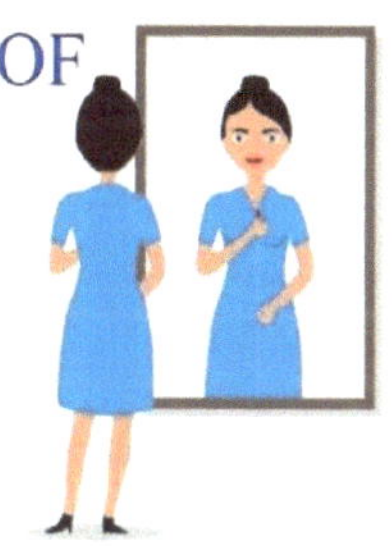

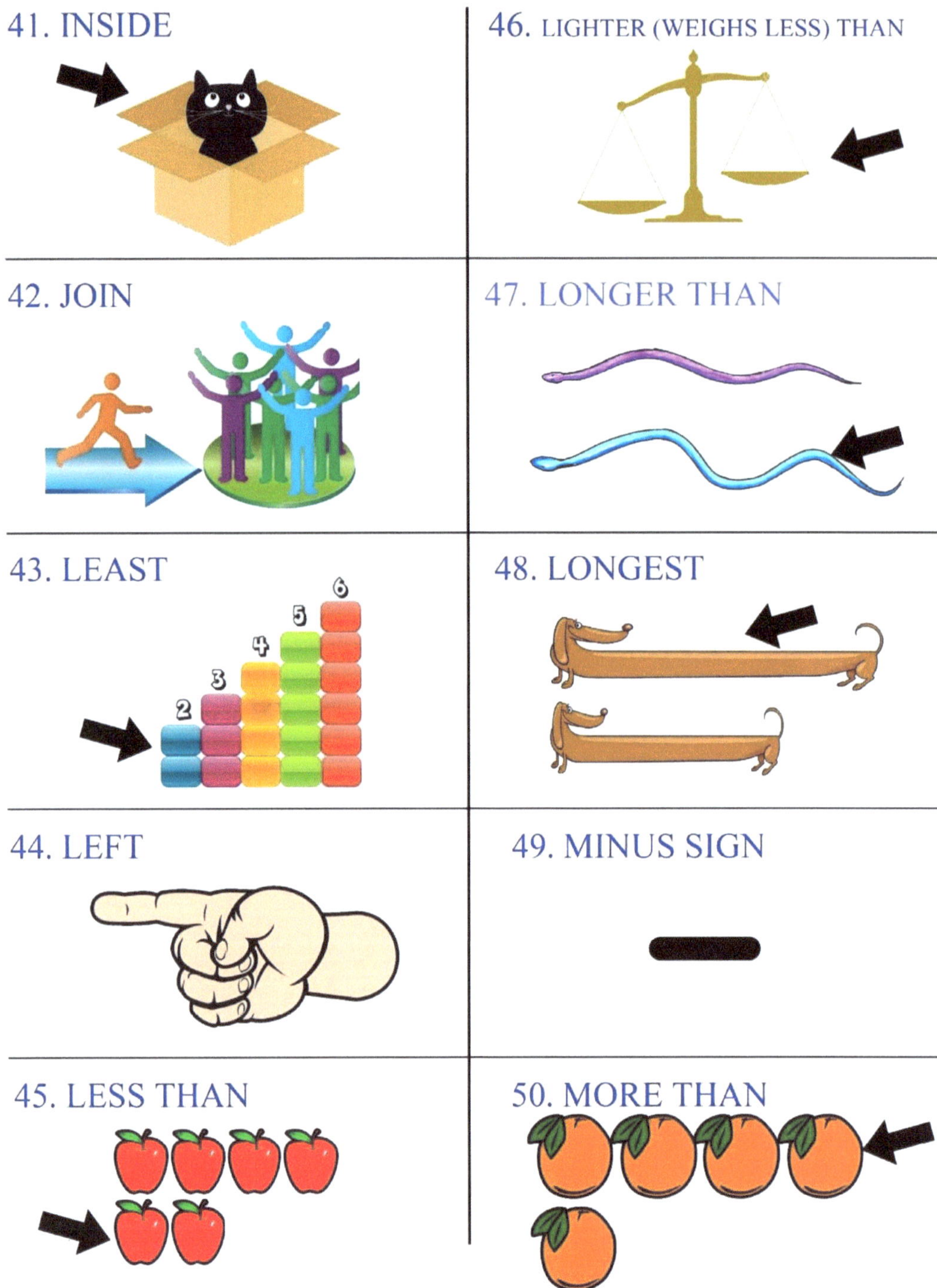

41. INSIDE
42. JOIN
43. LEAST
2 3 4 5 6
44. LEFT
45. LESS THAN
46. LIGHTER (WEIGHS LESS) THAN
47. LONGER THAN
48. LONGEST
49. MINUS SIGN
50. MORE THAN

51. MOST 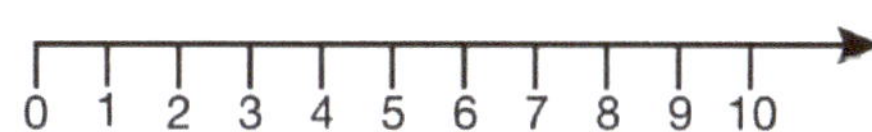	56. ORDER 
52. NUMBER LINE 0 1 2 3 4 5 6 7 8 9 10	57. OUTSIDE
53. NUMBER STORY 2 6 8	58. OVER
54. NUMBERS 	59. PART 
55. ON (ON TOP OF) 	60. PICTURE GRAPH 

61. PLUS SIGN	66. SAME

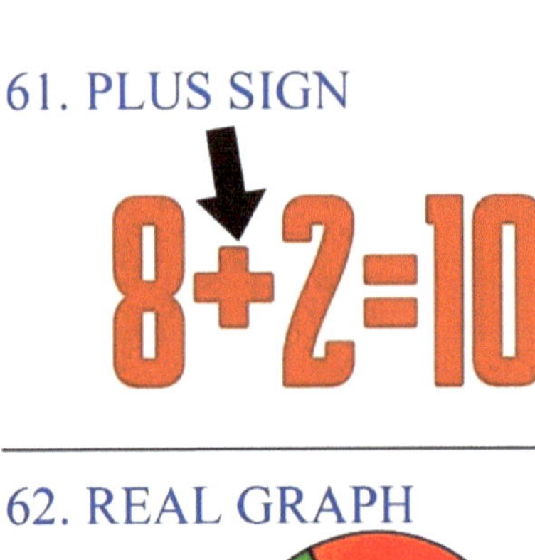

62. REAL GRAPH	67. SAME NUMBER AS

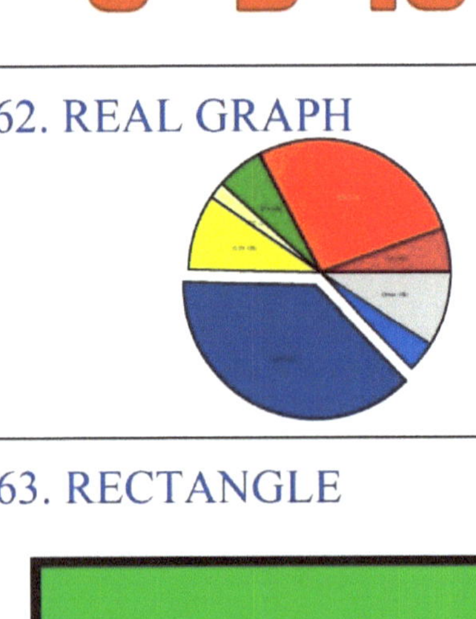

63. RECTANGLE	68. SAME SHAPE

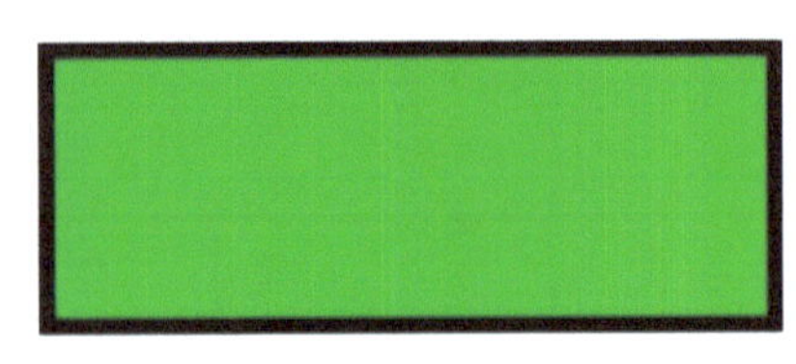

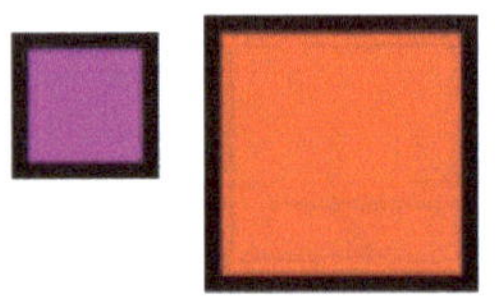

64. RIGHT	69. SAME SIZE

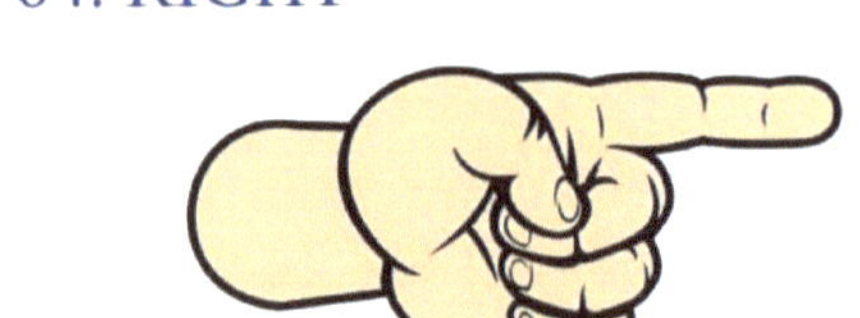

65. ROLL	70. SHORTER THAN

71. SHORTEST	76. SUBTRACT (TAKE AWAY)
72. SIDE	77. SUBTRACTION SENTENCE
73. SORT	78. SUM
74. SPHERE	79. TALLER THAN
75. SQUARE	80. TALLEST

81. TRIANGLE

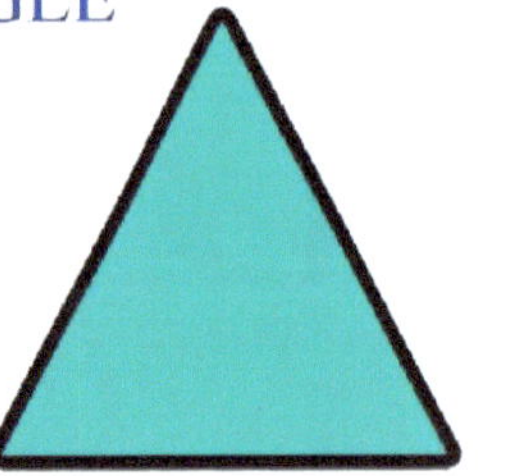

83. WHOLE

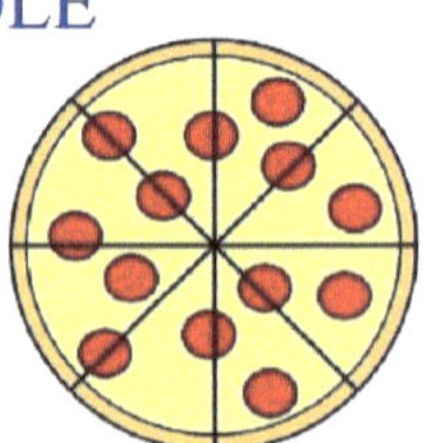

82. UNDER

Blank Word Cards

The following pages have the pictures without the words. Use them to assess your scholar's knowledge of the mathematical words.

Suggested use:

- Print out the cards and use them as flash cards.

- Ask the scholar to identify what word(s) are represented by the picture.

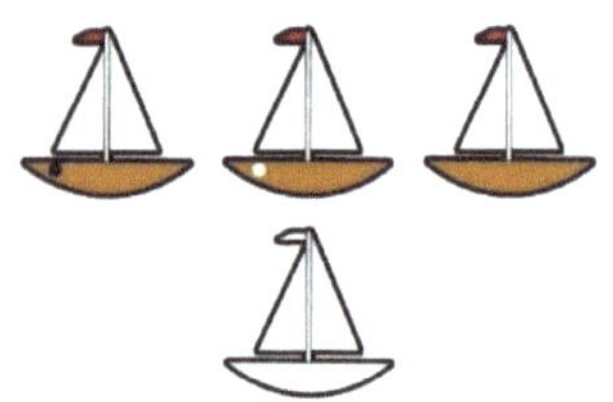

$3+2=5$

$9+2=11$

 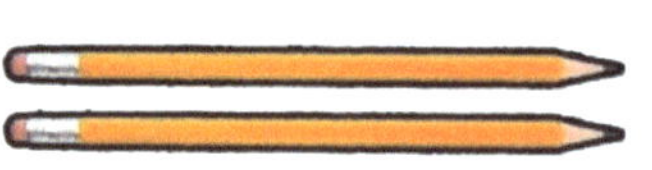

6   8   10   12   14   16

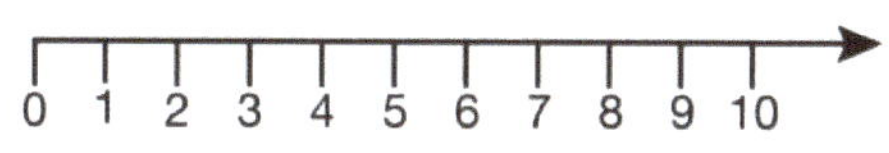

0 1 2 3 4 5 6 7 8 9 10

5-6-7-8-9

2 6 8

0 1 2 3 4
5 6 7 8 9

Fruit Collected
Banana
Apple
Cherry

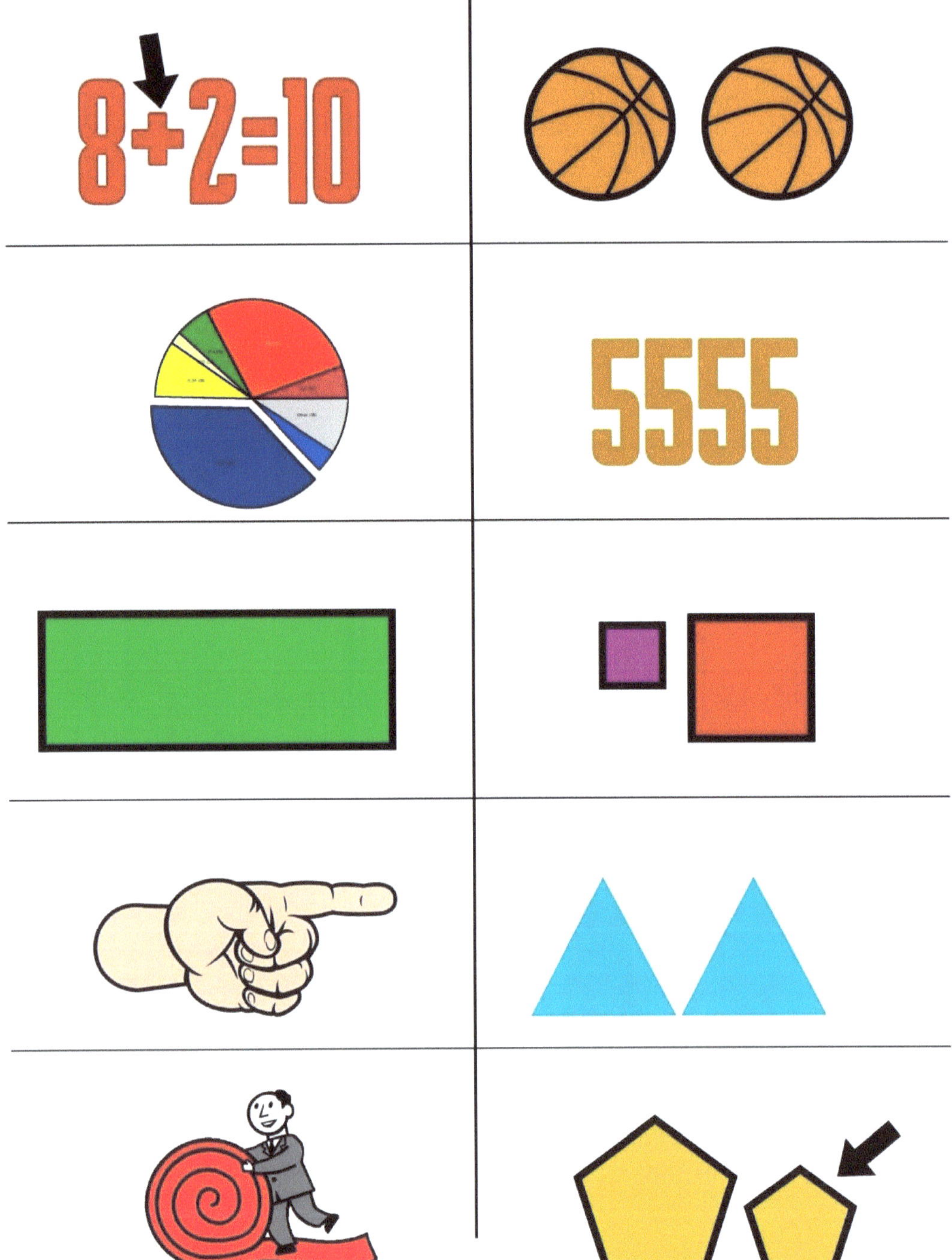

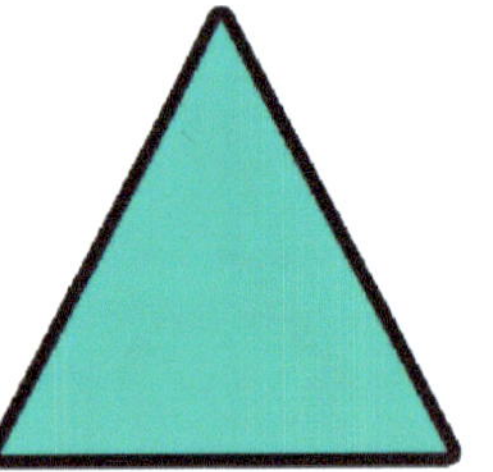

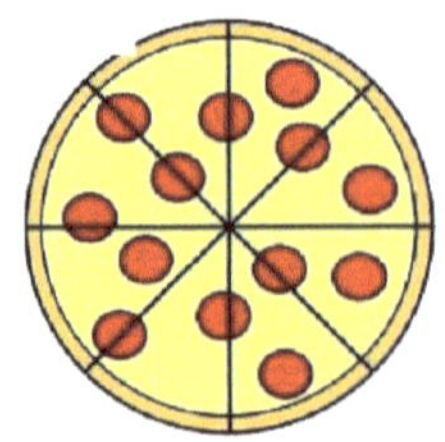

About the Authors

Dr. Edward C. Haynie holds a Bachelor of Science Degree in Chemistry and Mathematics, a Master of Science Degree in Chemistry, and a Doctor of Education Degree in Curriculum and Instruction/Science Education. Haynie has a vast and diverse background in science, which includes experiences in administration, teaching, research, planning, curriculum design and implementation of program in secondary schools, community college and university levels. He is also the Executive Director of the Incubator Scientist Program.

Lamar Hart received his Bachelor of Arts Degree in Computer Science with a minor in Mathematics from Saint Louis University. He is a current student at Grand Canyon University, where he is finishing his Master of Education Degree in Early Childhood Education. He has worked in the field of education for over fifteen years as an Information Technology Director and Computer Science teacher, a teacher assistant at Barack Obama Elementary School. He has also worked with Dr. Haynie with the Incubator Scientist Program for the past ten years.

www.ingramcontent.com/pod-product-compliance
Lightning Source LLC
Chambersburg PA
CBHW042124110726

48006CB00003B/751